How to Write Page-Turning Fiction

Advice to Authors

Helen Cox

Copyright © 2020 by Helen Cox. Published in the United Kingdom by Helen Cox Books

Ebook ISBN: 978-1-8380221-6-7
Paperback ISBN: 978-1-8380801-1-2
Hardback ISBN: 978-1-8380801-2-9

No part of this book may be used or reproduced in any manner whatsoever without written permission, except in the case of brief quotations embodied in critical articles or reviews. For further information visit helencoxbooks.com.

This book is written in British English.

Contents

1. INTRODUCTION	1
2. CHAPTER 1: PURPOSE	6
3. CHAPTER 2: GENRE	10
4. CHAPTER 3: TRANSFORMATION	15
5. CHAPTER 4: SHAPING CHAPTERS	21
6. CHAPTER 5: ARRIVE LATE, LEAVE EARLY	26
7. CHAPTER 6: I'LL NEVER TELL	31
8. CHAPTER 7: BEGINNINGS AND ENDINGS	36
9. CHAPTER 8: PLOTTING	43
10. CHAPTER 9: THE 21st CENTURY ARC	52
11. CHAPTER 10: THE UNREAL	62
12. CHAPTER 11: DIALOGUE	68
13. CHAPTER 12: TELLING DETAILS	74

14. CHAPTER 13: WALK AND CHEW GUM	78
15. CHAPTER 14: PAGE-TURNING SUPERPOWER	82
16. CHAPTER 15: THE EDITORIAL PROCESS	87
17. ACKNOWLEDGEMENTS	92
About the Author	93

INTRODUCTION

Before we get into what makes page-turning fiction, it is important to acknowledge the spirit in which this book is written. Technically speaking, there is no right or wrong way to compose and structure a story. That is perhaps why there are so many conflicting blog posts, podcasts and books about it. Every writer approaches the page from their own unique space. The techniques that have brought me nothing but artistic misery and failure may, for you, open up new avenues never before explored by fiction writers. In essence, what I'm saying is that this book is not designed to be prescriptive. Instead, my hope is that you will harness the approaches I've included for your own ends; use them as a springboard to leap to new horizons in your own creativity and service of a readership.

You may find that not all of the strategies explored are a fit for every story that you write. But I would argue most of them are worth considering if your aim is to engage a modern-day reader. Having taught many a creative writing class over the last decade, I have connected with numerous students who have suffered uncountable rejections from editors and agents, and they can't understand why. When I gently point out that it might be because the action doesn't really get started until chapter seven, they can become quite defensive and grope for some evidence that their approach is legitimate. Often, I will be told that Dickens or Austen or Orwell have employed the very same structure. And, as stated above, this is of course a creative choice. It is completely up to you as a writer if you wish to explore a story in this style. But reading and readers have changed considerably in the last hundred years. In the last thirty years, the rate of change in reading habits has only accelerated.

People writing decades, sometimes centuries ago, before the dawn of cinema, television and the internet had the luxury of taking their sweet time. The reader had little else to occupy them that wasn't work or socialising and even if they were a world class pianist or a dab hand at embroidery, these pastimes did not provide something very integral that human beings seem to thrive on: story and rich narrative. For that, a person either needed to turn to the champion orator in the family or to books. And not every family had a champion orator. In the 19th century or even in the pre-internet era, which I remember from my own youth, a book was wonderful solace during long, cold winters when outdoor activities were not possible. The modern-day writer is now vying for the attention of readers who have a surplus of literature at their fingertips. In addition to books, the number of films, tv shows, comics, computer games and online storytelling platforms available is staggering. In short, the modern-day reader has more stories available to them than they could ever hope to consume in one lifetime.

If we, as writers, want readers to choose our story over all the others they could be consuming, it would surely be unwise to test their patience by offering six chapters worth of preamble before the story really begins in chapter seven. In light of this argument, it is hopefully clear that this book is written with the intention of demonstrating how to best cater to a readership who are used to filmic, fast-paced storytelling. To satisfy readers who expect to be exhilarated from the first page, while taking into account genre expectations, which - I believe - apply to both genre and literary fiction.

Thus, while some might argue that these approaches stifle creativity or dilute voice as they encourage all fiction writers to adhere to certain principles, please be assured that is not my intention. On the contrary, I hope you find your own unique methods of twisting what I have written here. And when you do, I hope you write your own book about it so I can read it and the dialogue between writers can continue, and better stories can be written.

Before we get down to business, there is one last caveat worth mentioning. The approaches in this volume are not a magic formula that will make every reader who comes across your books love them. Crikey, if I had such a formula I could make us all very rich and happy off it. When it comes to storytelling, tastes vary wildly and it is therefore impossible to please everyone every time. Look at the online sales pages for my books and you'll find there are many 5-

star reviews in which the reviewers write that they read my book in one sitting, that they couldn't put it down, that they had to finish it even though it kept them reading long into the night or made them late for work. And yes, I love to see those because it means I have pleased another human being and brought them some joy. But there are also reviews from people who just didn't gel with my writing style. Who had hoped the story would go in a different direction, who had decided they didn't much like the principal character and consequently, that ruined the story for them.

This is a matter I discuss in more detail in my volume: How to *Become a Published Writer & Live to Tell the Tale* but as writers we cannot hope that our work will speak to everyone. If it did, the odds are it would be a fine example of mediocrity and little more. Though it is obviously our goal to make sure our books provide a pleasurable reading experience, we are not here to satisfy absolutely everyone of all tastes. What we can do is strive to streamline our storytelling approach in such a manner that it pleases most readers who like the kind of books we're writing – and maybe a few others who take a punt on us one slow Tuesday evening. I believe that employing the strategies in the following pages will help you do that. The chapters that follow are a culmination of every craft book, writing seminar and creative workshop I have ever read or attended as well as lessons I've learnt on the job writing novels, short stories and poetry for the last decade – and a bit.

CHAPTER 1: PURPOSE

Not to get all philosophical on you straight out the gate, but one of the most useful things you can do before writing fiction at any length is decide on your purpose. Why is it important to create this piece of work in the first place? Of all the writers in all the lands, why do you want to be the one to write this story? Why do you *need* to be the one to tell it? Why this story? Why now?

If you are interested in creative writing, you have probably come across the outliner/discovery writer debate. Or, as it's more commonly known, the plotter and pantser debate. Plotters being the kind of writers who like to pen an outline before they get started and pantsers being the kind of writers who 'fly by the seat of their pants' as they create. Engaging in this discussion in online forums is one of the many wonderful ways we distract ourselves from sitting down and actually writing our stories.

Hey, it beats doing the dishes.

People who lean towards discovery writing may not unravel their true purpose until they're near the end of the first draft, and certainly if that is your preference I'm not here to say you can't work that way and establish your purpose at a later point in the project. However, if you work this way you will probably need to prepare for some significant rewrites. Hate is a strong word but outliners such as myself do tend to hate rewrites. I will leave it to the reader to decide whether this is a sign of impatience or efficiency, but we tend to just want to get the story done. We want to get it down as best we can on a first sitting without too many pesky niggles to sort out when we're finished. And given my confession that I am an outliner at heart, it's perhaps not surprising that I'm starting this book by suggesting you consider your purpose from the outset. This, I have found, astronomically improves the chances of my finishing a book or short story to my satisfaction.

My recommendation is that you sit somewhere comfortable with your pen and notebook for just five minutes and ask yourself: *why do I want to tell this story?* If you can, write continuously for those five minutes, without stopping or overthinking, riffing on various ideas. Nobody is going to see this piece of writing. It's for your eyes only.

If you complete this task, the likelihood is you will come to at least a few conclusions about why your work is important. This can serve as a useful motivator, but don't be fooled into thinking you have to pick some great and lofty purpose. During the first UK Covid-19 lockdown, my purpose for writing romance and murder mystery novels was that I believed people needed to escape. I've had countless emails from readers who read my books during the numerous lockdown periods that explained how much they appreciated being transported out of a living situation none of us could really escape in physical terms.

Bringing solace to another human being was motivation galore for me. I wanted to make them laugh. I wanted to make them pine. I wanted to make them jump. Because I held that purpose firmly in my mind all the way through the writing process, that purpose shaped my work into something that was, for many readers, startling, seductive and page-turning.

I understand that discovery writers might be averse to deciding much of anything before they sit down to write a story but perhaps you could keep an open mind on this one? Or at least consider your purpose at the end of your first draft so that you can use it as a focus point during your rewrites. I promise it's not some philosophical exercise. I have genuinely found, time and again, that returning to this simple but integral detail is fundamental in crafting a story that readers can't put down. So often, it can help us determine what the overall theme or message of our piece is going to be and can even influence which elements from the writer's toolbox we utilise when telling our story.

Connecting with your purpose will also give your story something that many stories lack: real heart. Let's make no mistake about the fact that publishing is a business and fiction writers are often expected to write a minimum of two books a year, or many more short stories. As a result, some stories can feel somewhat 'churned out.' I bear no ill-will to writers who do churn out the odd story here and there. They do so because they are contracted to and because they won't get paid until they produce a fixed number of words. And just like you and I, these people have financial responsibilities. Still, I often think that churning feeling can be avoided by establishing your purpose from the outset. If your story has a deeper level and offers the reader a memorable, insightful or even inspiring experience, they are much more likely to keep turning those pages.

CHAPTER 2: GENRE

So much of providing a page-turning reader experience rests on considerations of genre. Consequently, understanding the genre you are writing in is, without doubt, a distinct advantage when crafting a story. Some writers believe genre to be too constricting and resist categorisation, wishing to write pieces that amalgamate several genres. While that is all well and good and you should be creative as you like, please do not overthink this part. Ultimately, whatever the dominant element is within your story is likely to dictate where bookshop owners and librarians place your books on the shelves and where editors place your work within a publication.

For those who find it rather callous to have their work pigeon-holed, there is, at least, some good news. You can actually make genre expectations work for you when writing your stories in ways that are guaranteed to inspire new readers to follow your work. Manipulating genre to create a story that readers just can't put down starts with considerable research. Out there, across the world, there are millions of people who belong to very specific readerships for very specific genres and expect very specific things from a particular kind of book. Though many consider literary fiction to be an outlier on this principle, I respectfully disagree. Even readers of literary fiction have expectations and a list of desirable story elements. For example, literary readers often expect an intense emotional or spiritual journey regardless of what other genres the book may straddle.

With this in mind, if you want to please that readership you need to get very familiar with that genre. If you don't do this not only do you minimise the chances of pleasing readers but you also minimise the chance of your book doing something new, inventive or unexpected. In short, it is difficult to offer your own unique twist on something if you don't know what it is you are twisting in the first place. Thus, I've come to believe that creating page-turning fiction is as much a research activity as it is a writing activity, particularly in the beginning but also likely as your story evolves.

For example, in the murder mystery genre in which I write, certain elements are expected such as a body, a sleuth who is a civilian investigator, clues and red herrings. Working on the principle that the mystery readers I'm catering to have read many hundreds of mysteries before mine however, I know I will need to find ways to twist those elements in my own unique way to save my book from appearing dull, trite or a rehash of what has gone before.

To achieve this, I might come up with a new murder method for my killer or dream up clues that have never before been used or offer the reader a red herring that goes completely against the usual stock characters they have become used to. Whichever slant I'm taking, I couldn't do so without first knowing what ingredients I was working with. Who are the stock characters? What clues are overused? Once I know this, I can make different creative choices that surprise and delight the reader. But I've got to do my homework first.

What ingredients are you working with in your genre? What has been done before many times over? When writing your story, how can you make these elements just different enough to add a new spark, a new energy and a new thrill for your reader? Can you combine elements from other genres to create a new hybrid genre that satisfies more than one readership? Although you want to keep some of the traditional tropes in place so that the book is recognisable to a readership, when you have been reading a genre for a long time, there are few things more exciting than an author who surprises you with a new take on an old convention that is clearly tailor-made for readers just like you.

Because of this, I would advise against writing in a genre that you don't read. I have always loved mystery, romance, fantasy and suspense. That's what I write because the research is then guaranteed to be fun. It gives me an excuse to work through my to-be-read list whilst exploring possibilities for new stories of my own. This is a wondrous way to spend your life: indulging in the kinds of stories you love most so you can create new ones that delight other people.

If you choose to write in a specific genre and do not read or, at the very least, consume stories through TV, comics and other media then the likelihood is you will create something that is a lot less original than you think it is, simply because you have no basis for comparison. When writing a mystery, you may choose to have all of your bodies turn up at abandoned fairgrounds. You might think this is super-original. But my question is, how will you know for sure? The straight answer is that you can't unless you've done some research and checked into what other writers are producing. It's the only way to be certain that twenty other mystery stories featuring abandoned fairgrounds haven't been released this year already.

Ironically, many authors have the reverse fear: the worry that reading in your genre will make you more derivative. Certainly, that was my fear to begin with when I started writing mysteries. I was petrified that I would accidentally steal a clue or a twist from one of the many books I had read or one of the many TV shows I had watched (seriously, I'm fairly sure I've seen every episode of Columbo at least three times it is so strangely interesting, but that's another story). Then I got wise and realised that even if one of my ideas did originate from reading a mystery, or watching one on TV, it would not be a carbon copy of that idea. It would be my own redeveloped twist on that original concept. The text that inspired me was really just a springboard; an example of what had gone before and an opportunity to build on that idea using different logic or perhaps setting up different reader expectations.

This revelation came as a tremendous relief as it meant I could again enjoy the stories I love so much and could consciously take inspiration from my literary heroes without worrying that I would duplicate their work. In truth, my mysteries have only become more elaborate and imaginative the more I have immersed myself in the genre. I can't say for sure that this will be your experience. I have however, shared this information with many of my creative writing students and witnessed first-hand the page-turning nature of their writing vastly increase the deeper they delve into their preferred genre.

Thus, my recommendation is not to be afraid of exploring the ground you're playing in. Instead, revel in every little detail, list your ingredients as you would a recipe, and decide how you are going to create your own unique story by mixing these ingredients together in a manner nobody else has before. And perhaps by adding a dash of something they're not expecting.

CHAPTER 3: TRANSFORMATION

One of the most regular questions I am asked in creative writing classes is: *where should I start my story? And, where should I end it?* We will drill down on the significance of beginnings and endings in writing fiction as this book progresses but the short answer to the question of where the overall structure for a story begins and ends is: it starts when change begins to happen and stops when a transformation is complete.

Before you start writing chapter one, I recommend considering the overall shape of your story. Before all the discovery writers throw this book across the room, let me at least qualify that I'm not asking you to plan the shape of the story in any great detail. I just want you to explore and understand one primary element: *what is the transformation? What change do we see between the first page and the last?* The more stories I have written, the more I've come to understand that narrative is, in essence, forward movement in a particular direction for both the characters and the world we are portraying on the page.

Fundamentally, I'm suggesting that your central character or the world they live in, or ideally both, should not be the same on page four hundred as they were on page one. Even cyclical narratives such as *Of Mice and Men* by John Steinbeck offer a shift for the central character. In the case of that book the character of George moves from trying to protect Lenny by keeping him alive to realising the only way he can protect Lenny from the world he lives in, and from himself, is to end his friend's life. It is a bleak and nuanced transformation but it is transformation none the less.

The unvarnished truth about storytelling is that stories that lack transformation often lack impact. This makes them very easy to spot. Have you ever finished watching a film or TV show or read a book and thought to yourself afterwards that something was missing? The characters might have been quirky and intriguing. The plot concept might have been unique. But when all said and done, something about it wasn't right. Something that you couldn't put your finger on? If you were pressed you might say it was the poor character development that stopped you from fully embracing that story. Or a lack of plot development. It's quite an odd human foible, but some part of us can sense when there isn't a reasonable amount of shift in a story. If the characters don't change, then we start to question whether or not the story has value.

I'm not suggesting it's impossible to tell a story where there is no change. It might be that you are attempting to show the inevitable endurance of a particular societal problem.

Certainly, not all of the characters in *Of Mice and Men* get transformations. But I would say such stories are the exception not the rule and even within those stories there will be some characters who do experience transformation, even if not everybody does, just so we can contrast them with characters who are stuck in a particular way of life without that hope of a change in fortunes.

This brings us back to the question: what transformation is at the heart of your story or stories? There are many journeys for a character to undertake from denial to acceptance; from selfishness to altruism; from cowardice to true bravery; from disconnection to connection. Because I'm one of those irksome optimists you meet from time to time, you can see I've ordered these journeys in such a way that they provide a happy ending. Just because I somehow ended up with the soul of an irrepressible Golden Labrador however, doesn't mean you have to structure your story the same way.

If you want to write a tragedy, just switch the journeys the other way around and portray your characters moving from light to darkness; from good to evil; from kindness to cruelty. These are not the stories I want to explore in my own books simply because I have found hope to be a very important thing to provide for readers when writing escapist fiction, but perhaps you would like to explore something different.

Some of our culture's most timeless stories are tragic.

Truly page-turning fiction tends to layer internal transformation with external transformation. For example, Star Wars is both a rite of passage story for Luke Skywalker and the story of how a small rebellion overcomes a huge galactic empire. At the beginning of the story, Luke is innocent of any power he might wield. By the end of the film, he has started on the journey to harnessing his true power as a Jedi. At the beginning of the story, the Empire is in complete control of the galaxy, save a few wayward rebels. By the end of the movie, the rebellion has struck a major blow to the Empire and taken a huge step forward in rebalancing power between good and evil. If Star Wars was only about one or the other of these things, it would be less compelling. It is the combination of internal and external transformation – made possible through conflict – that secures this film's status as one of the most-watched stories of all time.

Thus, to truly engage a modern-day audience with your stories, I would recommend selecting an internal and external shift for your characters and the world they live in. Amongst my published work are several murder mystery novels and when I'm writing those the external shift is easy: moving from a place of ignorance to knowledge; disorder to order. At the beginning, we don't know who killed the victim, and that person hasn't been brought to justice. In the end we do know who killed that person and they have been brought to justice. The element I always have to figure out when I am writing my murder mysteries is what the internal shift is going to be for the character who is at the centre of the mystery. I have played with all kinds of journeys for those characters including disconnection to connection; denial of our true self to acceptance of our true self; denial of our past to acceptance of our past and moving from feeling lost to finding a sense of direction. The list will go on. There are uncountable journeys for us and our characters to embark on. All we have to do is select the best journey for the plot we have in mind.

The rationale explored above is why I urge you, before you write your story, to take just a minute to ask yourself: *how will the character be different at the end of the story to the way they appear in the beginning? How will the situation be different at the end of the story when compared to the beginning?* As you write, bear that shape in mind all the way through because it will help you decide what events and twists and interactions should take place in your story. It will also ensure there is a clear thread running through your narrative and offers some excellent steer about how to start and what the ending should look like. In essence, the start of the story is the character's first step on the journey to transformation and the end is their last.

Regardless of whether you write an outline for your stories, knowing the overall transformation can be very useful if you ever get stuck and need to think through the next logical steps. If you have an overall shift in mind, in order to move forward you need only ask: *what is the next obvious step on that journey?*

CHAPTER 4: SHAPING CHAPTERS

All right. Enough sharing ideas about the preparation required before you start writing your story. Let's look at what needs to be considered when you do start writing (I can almost hear the discovery writers sighing in relief).

Many authors grasp the need for transformation in their work once the benefits of it have been pointed out, but what often takes more time to master is the granular use of shift and change from chapter to chapter or scene to scene. Establishing an overarching transformation within your story is valuable indeed, but it doesn't stop there. Ideally, forward movement should happen in every chapter or scene you write and that forward movement, or shift, should take the characters a step closer to their ultimate transformation.

Screenwriter Robert McKee advises that every scene must switch the polarity of a situation from positive to negative or negative to positive. Although this theory might sound like a somewhat simplistic way of looking at the smaller segments of our work, it does pay off as an approach to writing page-turning chapters.

Not convinced?

Think of it this way: if nothing changes between the opening of your chapter and the end of your chapter then there has been no development in the narrative – either of character or plot, when ideally you want to move both forward in every scene. Without this forward movement, your characters and your plot have essentially stalled and such moments can be highly hazardous for a writer trying to hold the attention of the modern-day reader. Some readers are more forgiving than others of course, but if your plot and character development has faltered, there is a strong chance that the reader will get bored, close the book, magazine or website and perhaps never return to it.

How do you put this polarity switch into action? Well, there is another, similar storytelling technique that I first heard from romance and YA author Nicola Doherty that can help with this. She referred to it as 'good news bad news' and fundamentally this approach echoes the idea of moving between positive and negative. It's perhaps most easily modelled through fairytale narrative given how simple and familiar those story structures are. As conflict often drives stories, it makes sense for us to start by delivering bad news to our character, and by proxy our readership.

Bad news Cinderella, your mother has died. But good news, your father is going to remarry and you are to have a new mother. But bad news, your new mother is cruel. But good news, there is going to be a royal ball. But bad news your mother forbids you from attending. But good news, your fairy godmother has the power to send you to this prestigious event. But bad news, you need to leave by midnight or everyone will know you are just a poor girl. But good news, the prince finds your slipper and searches for you across the land. But bad news, your step-sisters lock you away so you can't try on the slipper. But good news some helpful, animal friends free you, the slipper fits and you live happily ever after. In fairytales, characters often move from poor fortune to great fortune and the last segment of the story is often filled with nothing but good news.

Can you see how moving from good to bad news, from positive to negative and back again, keeps the story interesting? The reader wants to know if and how the outcome is ultimately going to be positive. Showing a character in their best and worst moments also aids the reader in forming a bond with them. They see the character in despair, and feel sympathy. Thus, when they see them move towards happiness, they begin to root for them.

The same approach can be used for even more compact moments in your story to heighten drama, tension and suspense. Let's take an example from one of my all-time favourite movies: *Die Hard* (Yes. I'd pick this over watching *Citizen Kane*, sorry). For those of you who are not aware of the plot, Bruce Willis plays a New York cop visiting LA who ends up trapped in a skyscraper under terrorist attack.

Well, actually they're not really terrorists, more thieves but we don't need to get into that. What you really need to know is that there comes a moment in which John McClane, the cop played by Bruce Willis, has no choice but to jump off the top of the skyscraper before the roof explodes, attached to the building by only a firehose... hey, we've all been there. This entire scene takes less than five minutes to play out but the use of 'good news bad news' makes it a gripping moment in the movie.

Bad news John McClane, you have to jump off the top of an exploding skyscraper with only a fire hose tied around your waist to stop your fall. But good news, you somehow survived that fantastical jump. But bad news, you didn't break the window when you swung into the building so you are stuck outside suspended hundreds of feet above the ground. But good news, you have a gun and can shoot your way through the window. But bad news, as you swing through the window, the fire hose container detaches from the roof and falls pulling you back towards the broken window where a fall of many stories awaits. But good news, you manage to untangle yourself just before you are pulled over the edge of the sill and plummet to your death.

Both the tale of *Cinderella* and John McClane's death defying skyscraper jump have gripped readers and viewers for centuries and decades respectively. They are both however, constructed on straightforward building blocks. These stories essentially juxtapose moments of hope and despair one after the other until either hope or despair wins out.

How can you make sure you're applying this approach effectively in your own story? You can often spot the moments in your manuscript where there is no shift because frequently this will be the moment where you find yourself getting a little bit bored when you're proofreading or revising your first draft. If this happens, even though you've read the story before, this should serve as a major warning sign. After all, I've read *Cinderella* dozens of times. I've watched *Die Hard* more than a hundred times (don't judge it's always on late night TV when you get back from the pub. Always). Am I bored with either of them?

Nope.

So, if you are reading your story for only a second time and find there are moments that drag, you need to take another look at what's happening there. After all, if you are bored a reader will be too. So, look at that part of your story again and see if there are ways in which you could better stimulate, intrigue and entertain the reader by introducing more shift, change and development to your chapter. More strategies on how to do that coming right up.

CHAPTER 5: ARRIVE LATE, LEAVE EARLY

Selecting a transformation for your overall story and ensuring transformation happens in each scene is a great starting point for creating page-turning fiction, but there are many more layers of storytelling to explore before we can say we've done everything we can to keep the reader hooked.

The following chapters outline certain techniques that I think will be of use when trying to achieve this, but to start off I'd like to focus on what I think is one of the most straightforward and effective methods of maximising the impact of whichever transformation you are working with. It is an approach that was taught to me by my friend and film critic, Nigel Floyd. He said to me once: *'what so many storytellers don't understand is that in every scene they should arrive late and leave early.'* I remember being struck by the simplicity and obvious power of this statement and told him as much at the time how clever I thought it was. On some level, I had known this throughout my writing career. The general idea absorbed through the many stories I'd consumed. But I'd never heard anyone put it in such a way that enabled me to so readily action the technique in my own work. If you're not sure what Mr Floyd meant by this, allow me to elaborate.

If you are writing a scene about an argument at a dinner party, we do not need to see the central character get in the car to go to the dinner party. Or the drive there. Or the character pulling up to the house where the dinner party will take place. Or even the character knocking on the door. Instead, you can bring us in right when the first confrontational event happens at the dinner table. It might be somebody saying something rude or a party guest becoming violent or engaging in uncouth, drunken behaviour. Whatever it is, start the scene there.

I know you think you need all that previous characterisation but in truth, we will be able to tell who everybody is at that table by their reaction to this conflict. We will understand immediately how confident they are, how brave, how judgmental and if you want to throw in a few more details about body language and physical appearance that can help too. But when adversity comes knocking, people tend to show their true colours. This philosophical truth gives the writer permission to start their story in the midst of the conflict and subsequently show who the characters are from their reaction alone. Yes, we will undoubtedly learn more about these characters and the situation as the story progresses but conflict offers the reader an immediate sense of the players in the story while also building intrigue over what will happen next.

Similarly, at the end of a chapter, and at the end of a story, it is better to leave early than outstay your welcome with the reader. If you've tied up the major transformation, you don't need to tie up every other last detail. Anyone who has seen the third instalment of *The Lord of the Rings* movies, *Return of the King* will understand what I mean by this. That film has approximately seven different endings. It is the guest who doesn't know when it has outstayed its welcome. Most of what we are shown at the end of that trilogy is unnecessary and most viewers could have figured out all that closure for themselves. Don't get me wrong, there was a lot of very entertaining stuff in the preceding nine hours. But that ending could have been much sharper and was perhaps more dictated by an attempt to please too many factions of *Lord of the Rings* fans than it was by good storytelling form.

Just as the notion of transformation applies to both the overall story and individual chapters then, so too does the 'arrive late, leave early' guideline. If you keep this strategy at the forefront of your mind during the writing of pieces long or short, you will keep your pages action-packed; filled with only the most crucial, intriguing, and entertaining information. In short, there will be no fat to trim.

Whenever we are considering using a particular strategy in our work, it's always wise to look at its possible limitations. This principle can be used pretty broadly without any hitches but how far you take it is going to be in some part dictated by genre, and whether you are writing in a series.

To offer an example, I knew my first cosy mystery novel would be part of a long-running series and that readers expected to be made, er, well, cosy before the grittier aspect of a murder was introduced. Consequently, I had to weigh this against my desire to get the action started as soon as possible and allowed myself to use the entirety of the first chapter for exposition only. To ensure the reader was properly acquainted with the regular cast of characters and that they could visualise the setting in detail. Book two of the same series, was written from the perspective of another character. Thus, I again used the first, slightly shorter, chapter for setting up the next mystery from this new perspective. By book three in the series however, readers knew the characters and understood that the perspective would switch in each subsequent instalment. This meant I could happily set-up the central mystery on the very first line. While some people may choose to read that book as a stand-alone, most people reading that series are reading it in sequence, so I knew I was on safe ground with this tactic.

Usually, I would not spend so much time on set-up in my fiction work as I did with this series - though I suppose for the forgiving reader a chapter isn't really that long at all. I constructed the story this way because I knew that within the cosy mystery genre, readers often prefer books that start at a somewhat gentler pace. If I was writing a high-octane thriller series, I would come in hard and fast with the central conflict on the very first line and trust my reader to catch-up with the characters, backstory and setting as the action unfolded. That would be what such readers are used to and indeed what they would expect. But this guideline is elastic depending on genre and whether you are writing a standalone novel. As the author, you know your story and your characters better than anyone else. You therefore have the authority to adapt this approach to different degrees depending on the narrative you are building.

CHAPTER 6: I'LL NEVER TELL

I'm about to tell you something revolutionary.

So please don't freak out, OK?

Because I know you've probably read ten or twenty how-to writing guides or been to five or ten writing workshops where you are told explicitly, in no uncertain terms, that no matter what happens you must never, ever, ever tell.

Ever.

Many a creative writing tutor and seasoned author will have told you that true writers do not tell. They show the action and let their readers draw their own conclusions. This is a tenet of craft development that has been around for so long now that only a select few have dared question it. But as creative people, it does not serve us to deal in absolutes. Arguably what serves creative folk best however is keeping an open mind and never outright dismissing anything. In fact, a bit like the mischievous child who just has to go and do the one thing they are told not to do, sometimes going against all guidance and experimenting with forbidden techniques can have interesting and powerful effects on the page.

Now, I'll admit, on the whole, I'm very much in favour of showing. I think the average reader prefers to see the action play out rather than be told it second-hand by a narrator. But it is important to note that this is a huge generalisation. Under certain circumstances, it is totally fine to tell. When editing manuscripts I frequently come across portions of a story that have been shown simply because the writer is taking the advice they've been given a step too far.

This is not to say you shouldn't show all the important stuff; the interactions that are really at the core of the plot and the characterization. Yes, we want to see that shown, with the real-time reactions of all the characters. But there are some smaller episodes that can be briefly summarised by telling. Sometimes these episodes are required for continuity or to offer an abridged account of an uneventful period in a character's life because though nothing significant happened to them it is important for the reader to understand that time has passed.

In comic book terms, these episodes are all the things that happen between the frames. i.e. We see Batman take down those robbers. But between that frame and the next, the likelihood is Bruce Wayne goes home, puts the kettle on and curls up in his Batcave with a cup of tea and his favourite binge-worthy Netflix show and, frankly, we don't need to see that. In comic books the time between Batman taking out those robbers and the next sequence of action is often simply connoted with a sentence like 'The next day…' and that's enough for us. We understand that a chunk of time has passed and that nothing too eventful happened between this frame and the last, otherwise we would have been shown those events in the frames.

We can use the same approach to present similar shifts in novels and short stories. Consider these lines from the opening of the sixth chapter in my historical romance novella: *Disarming the Wildest Warrior*:

Four days passed before Blue Sky had any business visiting Gilda Griffiths. Four endless days of busying himself with hunting, fishing and shooting arrows into practice marks so he might forget the fire that had at once ignited within when she threw her arms around him and nestled her precious little head into his chest.

This is all telling, but it is legitimate telling. Firstly, because I need the reader to understand that Shawnee warrior Blue Sky has pined for Gilda for four days. I need the reader to know that he cannot get this woman off his mind even when he hasn't seen her for a good long while. But, I can't show those four days for one very good reason: romance readers are reading because they want to see the couple together, interacting and getting to know each other. Thus, in a forty thousand word romance novella, I do not have the word count space to keep them apart for long at all.

Yes, I could have included an entire chapter in which we saw Blue Sky back at his village. Talking to a friend who knew he had been captivated by this woman, while he shot arrows into practice marks and engaged in the other distractions listed. I could have included this to underline to the audience how hard he was trying to forget this woman, and there wouldn't per se be anything wrong with that.

Except that it would keep my two love interests apart for another chapter and I know my readership want to see the characters together.

And, because I knew the shape of my story from the outset I also knew that my two central characters would be separated for a chapter at the mid-point and for a couple of chapters later in the book as I built towards the climax of the plot. That's quite a lot of time for the love interests to be apart in a romance novella.

Thus, earlier in the book, I had to make sure they were only apart when it was absolutely necessary to drive forward their ultimate transformations. When I examined my structure with this in mind, it was easy to see that I had no legitimate reason to include that extra scene at Blue Sky's village. My strategy was and remains to curate only the most active and emotional moments for my readership as appropriate to expectations for that genre. To essentially deliver only the moments a reader in this genre wants to partake in, with perhaps one or two surprises thrown in to keep things fresh. Any gaps between those moments can be bridged with brief moments of telling. In most cases a story will be better for that creative cut.

This is an approach you can adopt in your own stories: to learn what is most important to your readership in the genre you are writing in. Then select which material to include. This way, you ensure you show the scenes your readership are most interested in and briefly summarise those that are less interesting to them through telling. Getting those things the wrong way round probably wouldn't be a good look and would undoubtedly make it less likely that readers will come back for more of your stories. There are lots of online communities out there that encourage interaction between readers of particular genres. If you engage with your proposed readership in such communities, it stands to reason that you will get a much better grasp of which story elements you can afford to summarise for the sake of pace and brevity.

CHAPTER 7: BEGINNINGS AND ENDINGS

I wonder how many times I sat in a creative writing class in the early days of my career and was told by a seasoned writer that I needed to make the first line of my stories 'work hard.'

Dozens of times at least.

Not once, however, was that idea broken down into practical terms, even when I asked if they'd mind explaining it a little more. On some level, I sort of understood what was meant by this instruction. My first line had to be intriguing. It had to grab the reader. But those are also quite vague phrases and, being a practical person at my core, I needed more specific advice.

After years of practice, I've got a grip on this concept but rather than just repeat to you that your first line needs to 'work hard', I want to break down how you actually make it work hard when it comes to commandeering the attention of your readership.

When readers start reading a story, they are pretty much clueless about all the fundamental aspects of the narrative:

the who, the what, the where, the when, the how and the why. Yes, they may have some idea of the story from the title, the front cover or the blurb if it's a novel or short story collection in book form. But these elements are designed to sell the book, not necessarily to tell the story. Consequently, if anything, the reader might come to the story with a slightly false impression based on these elements alone. A strong first line however will establish, or at least drop hints about, several of the who, what, where, when how and why elements so that the reader immediately has something concrete to connect with.

Take this opening line, again from my romance novella: *Disarming the Wildest Warrior*:

The heart-stopping howl of a man in torment was the first thing Gilda Griffiths heard when she stepped off the coach at Williamsburg.

When writing this line, I had to consider which elements of the story were most important. The 'when' had already been covered by inserting the date '1725' at the top of the page above the chapter heading. As this is a historical romance story, the 'when' is of utmost importance. Thus, I didn't even wait for the first line to convey that to readers. Instead, I signposted the date using a large heading so that readers knew which period in history they were about to become immersed in. With the 'when' taken care of, I then turned to the other fundamental elements that I had to choose from.

If I tried to incorporate all of them in a first line then it would become a ridiculously long sentence. It would throw too much information at the reader at once and that is more likely to be off-putting than intriguing. There's a careful balance to be struck here. If all of your questions about what kind of story this is going to be are answered in line one, why would the reader bother reading on? Some readers might continue but if the rest of your readership think they can predict every twist and turn in the story before they've read three sentences, they may move onto other stories that hold back just enough to maintain an air of mystery.

In the case of this novella I decided to focus on the where, the who and the what. The 'what' is often the conflict so wherever possible I like to include that in my first line. In this case, the 'what' is a 'heart-stopping howl' that connotes suffering and possible peril. This conflict is what at once pulls Gilda (the 'who') into the path of her future lover: Blue Sky. The man in torment is Blue Sky's father. All of this other information is established later in the chapter, once we have seen how Gilda responds to the man in torment and established her as a central figure in the story who is compassionate and a skilled physician. I also included the 'where' in the first line so that readers could connect it with the 1725 date at the top of the page and understand, at once, that this was a love story set in colonial America.

You'll notice there is nothing particularly 'clever' about this first line.

Yes, 'heart-stopping howl' is alliteration but I'm hardly going to win any literary awards for that. This sentence conveys essential information simply so that it remains accessible to a wide range of readers. Its primary function is to ensure enough detail is established in this first line for readers to orientate themselves within the world of the story. In addition to all the elements listed above, there is also a reference to a physical journey which foreshadows the emotional journey this character will take. If you can allude to a shift, change or journey in the first sentence this is often very useful as it subtly sets up the narrative arc – the transformation the character will undergo by the end of the story.

Applying these principles to the opening of your story and ensuring the most useful information is established up front, while hinting at the journey ahead, creates a strong start for your story. But it doesn't stop there. If this approach of starting strong works at the very beginning of your story, then why would you only use it once? In my own work I use this approach at the beginning of every single chapter or scene by considering: what is the fundamental information that needs to be conveyed here? What transformation will happen in this sequence and how can I hint at it in the first line? Because of this, every time I write a new sequence or chapter the opening packs a punch and renews the energy of the piece I'm working on. If every chapter opening or scene opening is as intriguing as the first, it makes it very difficult for the reader to put the story down – which of course was our not-so-evil plan all along.

As we all know, however, stories and chapters don't just have openings, they have endings too. Knowing how to end a story or chapter is often just as much a conundrum to the beginning writer as starting them is. For if we do not find a way to close chapters and stories in a way that makes people want to keep reading, then they may never get to chapter two. Moreover, they may never read another short story or buy another book from us.

And this would be sad.

There are lots of people in the writing community who talk about how to structure an ending but the master is surely James Scott Bell who wrote a whole book on how to write unforgettable endings entitled: *The Last Fifty Pages: The Art and Craft of Unforgettable Endings*. I have read several of Bell's books and listened to much of his audio output but probably the nugget that resonated with me most was his discussion of what he called 'prompt lines'. This is essentially a last line in a chapter that leaves an element of the narrative uncertain so that the reader has to turn the page to find out what happens next. Here's an example of a prompt line from the first chapter of my cosy mystery novel: *Murder on the Moorland*.

'Exactly what Halloran would do when he once again came face to face with his wife's killer, he hadn't yet decided.'

My readership with this series has followed my librarian sleuth Kitt Hartley and her new boyfriend DI Halloran for three books so this prompt line carries quite a lot of weight for them. After reading this line, not only will they want to know what actions Halloran *does* take when facing down the man who killed his wife but they also want to know how this will impact his relatively fresh romantic relationship with Kitt.

Essentially, if you want to guarantee that your reader will turn the page into the next chapter, then the chapter they have just finished cannot end on a note of complete fulfilment. There needs to be a suggestion of, and space for, more. Until you finish the book or story, there has to be something left unsaid, uncertain and unknown. As long as there is some uncertainty and the characters are ones the readers can invest in they will keep reading. Even when finishing your book, if it is part of a series you may want to offer the reader a 'HFN' – Happy For Now scenario rather than a happily ever after to indicate that there is still yet more to discover in future books while simultaneously offering readers satisfaction on whatever chief conflict was addressed within this story.

Looking at structure at this granular level and thinking more carefully about the shape of our chapters, as well as the overall shape of the story, is more likely to help us produce addictive content for our readership. It's a model that is used in many an addictive Netflix series designed for some serious binging and it is a model we can welcome into our own writing, when appropriate to our genre, to entice readers to choose our story above all others available to them.

CHAPTER 8: PLOTTING

So many writers get all turned about when it comes to plot structure and for a number of years I was no exception. Over the time I've been writing however, I've come to understand a straightforward, angst-free approach is the best ticket to getting your story finished and in the hands of readers.

Sometimes, I believe our instinct is to overcomplicate plotting as, despite the number of craft books we read, a small part of us believes that it is specialist knowledge that only a favoured few understand how to manipulate to resounding success. Though engaging with academic ideas about narrative structure regularly is likely to enrich your understanding, and your craft, in essence, storytelling is a pretty primal activity for us. We tell stories all the time and, generally, they comprise a set-up, a major incident and a conclusion. Put simply: a beginning, a middle and end.

Once you have these things figured out, you can manipulate the delivery of these elements anyway you want. You can bring us in at the conclusion and flashback to the beginning so we can see how things turn out that way. You can create a non- linear narrative that hops back and forth in different timelines for each character. But deciding where the story starts, what happens in the middle and what happens in the end is the foundation. And, if you've taken the time to select an overarching transformation for your character then you've already got the fundamentals of plotting down because it will be that transformation that drives the story. That transformation will also dictate where the story starts, where it ends and what kind of stuff you need to put in the middle.

If you're looking to add more layers or more definition to the story you've created, I would recommend starting with a closer examination of your central character. They are, after all, the principal player in whatever plot you've designed and can be the key to unlocking some truly page-turning elements you may otherwise have neglected to include. In addition to establishing the core transformation, try asking yourself the following questions about your central characters:

What is your character's greatest strength?

What is your character's greatest weakness?

What is your character's greatest desire?

What is your character's greatest fear?

If you know the answers to these four questions, then you have the information you need to further refine your story into a yarn readers can't get enough of. A character's desire starts them on the path of transformation. If you are writing an optimistic story, the character's strength carries them through their transformation. If you are writing a tragedy, a character's weakness propels them towards their transformation – often alongside their desire for something immoral or extreme.

It is possibly their greatest fear however, that can be most easily utilised to add page-turning elements to your story. Offering the most basic example, if, like Indiana Jones, your central character is petrified of snakes, at some point you just have to throw them into a big pit of snakes.

After all, which is going to be more riveting? Watching a person who is a bonafide snake charmer find their way out of a pit of snakes or watching someone who is scared to death of snakes find their way out of a pit of snakes? This goes for any fear your character might have, be it physical, emotional or spiritual.

In romance, the character's biggest fear is frequently the fear of intimacy. Of being vulnerable and letting someone in. Until The Perfect Person For Them enters their life. The one person who they are willing to risk it all for even though they may spend the vast majority of the word count conflicted about whether the payoff is worth any pain attached to the coupling.

Your character might be afraid of anything: heights, balloons, rubber ducks, Chuck Norris, abandonment, loneliness, heartbreak, bereavement, and the list goes on. When you fully investigate this truth about your character, you will have the information you need to insert some entertaining, terrifying or exhilarating episodes into your story, all of which move your character closer to their transformation in one way or anothe. For when we shift into a different space from the one we inhabited before, we inevitably have to face our fears.

Moving beyond character and looking at the technicalities of structure, there are lots of different models for plotting out there but in my experience it is hard to beat the three-act structure. It fits the beginning, middle and end model all too neatly even if, as I explained before, you choose to deliver the acts in a non-linear fashion or use flashback.

Get your story straight first, then you can jumble it up to your heart's content.

I must admit, however, that when I first came across the three-act structure many, many years ago, I didn't feel the finer points were conveyed to me in accessible terms. Considering one of the criticisms of the three-act structure is that it is 'too formulaic' it is quite astounding that this simple 'formula' couldn't be easily translated to a newbie writer. Maybe I was just a bit slow (some of my school reports certainly suggest it). But I know from conversations with other writers then, and many I have had since, that I wasn't alone.

Allow me to try and rectify this now.

The big difference between talking about the beginning, middle and end and the three-act structure is the two major 'turning points' for the central character at the end of act one and the end of act two. Both of these turning points propel the character into the final, climatic ending.

Initially, I found these turning points a tad confusing. What were they in real terms? Over the time I've been writing I've come to understand that they are better described as two major steps towards the ultimate transformation, rather than turning points. Turning point suggests an about turn of some kind when in fact, although the turning point is likely to be a setback of some nature, it is a setback that ultimately generates forward movement. These points in the story are a bit like when an archer draws back the string on their bow. The arrow is momentarily pulled backwards but then propelled forward at incredible speed in whichever direction it is aimed.

Such concepts are often best understood when they are modelled.

Just as I used *Cinderella* to model the 'good news, bad news' approach earlier, I am now going to turn to the best-known version of *Beauty and the Beast* to model the three-act structure due to the story's simplicity and familiarity.

Every single incident in the first act of *Beauty and the Beast* is leading to a major turning point for the central character of Beauty. This turning point happens when she agrees to take her father's place as the Beast's prisoner and thus sacrifices her own future. This altruistic act will forever change the course of both her life and the life of the Beast. All the smaller events that happen in act one lead to this fateful moment.

As the second act progresses, however, what Beauty believed would be a major life setback turns out to spark an unusual relationship with her captor.

One that intrigues both she and the beast. As the relationship develops, all of their actions lead to the major turning point at the end of act two: the moment when the Beast releases Beauty so she can go to the aid of her father. In the space of act two, the Beast has learnt vulnerability and sacrifice. He sacrifices his own happiness for Beauty's.

When the Beast lets Beauty go, again it seems to him like a terrible blow. He does not believe he will see the one woman he loves ever again. Ultimately, however Beauty and the Beast have their happy ending because they both braved their own turning points in the story which both ultimately lead to the climactic finale in which the villagers storm the Beast's castle and the Beast's curse is broken via Beauty's love for him.

This, in a nutshell, is the three-act structure and if your primary goal is to create something truly page-turning for your reader, you don't need to look much further than this structure for your foundation. It is a structure that is familiar to us whilst still allowing for some surprises which is perhaps why it is so widely used and why readers respond so well to it. This structure is so fundamental to storytelling that many other models that profess to be vastly different to the three-act structure, such as the hero's journey, roughly follow the same rhythm (read Christopher Vogler's *The Writer's Journey* for more information on that).

Understandably, many writers who use this structure get stuck around the middle way point because the distance between those two crucial turning points is quite some way and sometimes we can't see a clear roadmap between one turning point and another. In such instances, I often advise fellow writers, and my creative writing students, to use the 'good news, bad news' technique explained previously so that they can hop from one incident to the next knowing that their characters will face both hope and despair on the path between those major points of transition.

This remedy often works because 'good news, bad news' grips readers and ensures the story is laced with conflict the central character has to overcome in order to win out in the end. Or, with tragedy, a conflict they perhaps try to overcome and fail. If you want to make your story significantly lighter or darker, simply alter the ratio of good news to bad news. In a lighter story try 'good news, good news, bad news.' In a darker story try 'bad news, bad news, good news.' I know that this might seem simplistic but it is incredible what can come out of the storytelling process when we focus on simple principles such as these rather than become despairing as we try to navigate complicated structures that don't necessarily add anything particularly significant to the process.

A further approach that may help you keep momentum between the end of act one and the end of act two is to consider the following questions whenever you get stuck: what would my character hate to happen next? What would force them to take one more step in the direction they really don't want to go in? This is useful because often, to add more conflict to our stories, we make our central character a reluctant player in their own transformation.

If there was a mechanism by which you could speak to the character of Beauty at the beginning of the story, she would probably tell you she would not want to fall in love with a beast. But that is exactly what she does. If you could address the Beast at the beginning of the story, he would probably tell you he doesn't want to fall in love at all – even if it means breaking the curse, it also means intimacy. Putting another person before yourself and risking your heart. But again, he takes that risk even if it's the last thing he feels comfortable doing. They are both forced along a path they would not choose but is, in truth, the key to their ultimate fulfilment. What is the key to your character's fulfilment? And what would force them to take steps towards that resulting transformation?

Besides the above, you can also question what your readership would most want to see happen next. Then decide if you are going to deliver it straight away or tease them with slightly delayed gratification to keep them reading for longer. It's a delicate balance. Keep them waiting too long and they may lose patience. You can discover whether you've left the reader hanging a bit too long by getting feedback on your manuscript from Beta Readers. And if you strike the balance just right there is little doubt that your reader will be up late reading long into the night, and have you to thank for their tiredness the next day.

CHAPTER 9: THE 21ST CENTURY ARC

Traditionally, when people talk about an 'arc' in relation to fiction they are referring to a character arc. Which is essentially the transformation that I wrote about at the beginning of this volume.

During my time teaching creative writing, and writing for myself, however I have developed an ARC acronym that I believe to be a useful construct for authors writing for the 21st Century audience.

Let me start this portion of the book by saying that I think stories are very powerful. Perhaps that's not so surprising given that I write stories for a living. And given that every spare second I get when I'm not writing, I'm reading them. But I truly believe that if we tell the same stories repeatedly they become part of our reality and not always in a good way.

In real life, away from the world of fiction, there are stories surrounding all kinds of issues in our society. About people from particular cultural backgrounds. About men. About women. About those who identify as non-binary. About people from particular classes. About victims of particular crimes. The list goes on. You don't need me to identify examples, I'm sure you read the headlines just as well as I do. You know what I'm talking about.

You may also remember that at the beginning of this book I stated that this volume was designed to help writers serve a 21st Century readership. In order to truly achieve this, I believe we need to subvert the stories that have gone before. We need to make space on the page for new characters who haven't been acknowledged in the past and readdress some imbalances in all the literature that has gone before. For I'm pleased to say that the world has changed and people who were less visible, had fewer rights, were left unheard are becoming visible, are gaining rights and are at long last being listened to. We can increase the visibility of such people and the issues surrounding this shift if we choose to write different stories.

The acronym I've developed, the 21st Century ARC, is designed to tell those stories. To offer writers and readers a fresh focus. We need to breathe new life into what has gone before. So, this approach is two-pronged in its purpose: first, it highlights our responsibilities as writers to create more inclusive material and secondly, it adds a subversive element to our stories that readers are likely to find compelling – offering you yet more page-turning clout.

Let's explore each letter of the ARC acronym in turn.

A is for agency. Who are you giving the agency to in your stories? Who has the power to change their own destiny and that of others? Who saves the day? Who has all the solutions?

Traditionally in western literature, this agency would be given to a white, straight, able-bodied male. They would be the ones tasked to be the hero. To make the sacrifice. To solve all problems. Not only does this not allow any space for other more diverse heroes of different mental health statuses, physical abilities, racial backgrounds or sexualities, it is also a painfully unfair story to keep telling ad infinitum. Like I said, if we tell the same story again over and over, it can become part of our reality. The idea that men have to be strong heroes with the solution to all problems is one of those dangerous stories we have been telling far too long.

You don't have to take my word for it. Just look at male suicide rates in any country in the western world. Equating a man's worth with his bank balance, employment status and ability to provide is a narrative that is killing our men alongside limiting the life choices of women and non-binary individuals. I, for one, am not willing to keep writing stories that perpetuate that narrative. I will continue to write stories and books where men are allowed to not have the answers. Where someone else shares the burden of saving the day, or takes it out of their hands completely. I write stories in which men are permitted to be vulnerable and all other characters regardless of how they identify have the opportunity to step forward and claim their space in whatever battle is being fought.

You may feel differently. You may be more interested in interrupting or contradicting other repeated stories – and that's fine. There are plenty of dangerous stories our society tells to choose from. But many of them can be challenged by the simple act of changing who has the agency in your story. Who has the power to initiate positive change?

I recommend bestowing the agency in your story on someone who usually stands on the sidelines and make them active players in their own destiny. This doesn't mean that they make all the right choices (there probably isn't much of a story in that) but that they take action towards a goal, dream or desire. Naturally, there are forces in the world that are bigger than us and push us in a certain direction. That doesn't mean that your characters have to become passive pawns. Write characters that push back. Write characters that react when they're not supposed to and get themselves into fixes. Show us that the protagonist has some ideals, principles and plans of their own. Show us they've got attitude.

R is for representation. This is a slightly more complicated area than that of agency, because even though I've suggested above that you should give your agency to somebody in your list of characters who normally would be overlooked, the last thing I'm recommending here is that you lapse into tokenism. i.e. including a character from a different background / sexuality / age range in your story just to give the illusion of representation. If those characters don't have a real journey or an essential contribution to make to the plot, they are just two-dimensional vehicles and nothing more. Ideally, you will show us the body, heart and soul of those people in Technicolor and surround sound. Explore how their mental health status, their background, their age, their sexuality, affects their relationships in a sensitive and compassionate manner. The barriers they face, the connections they create. Do this, and your fiction will much better reflect the reality we live in – even if it's a fantasy story!

Alongside the concern of tokenism, some writers steer away from writing more representative stories because they are understandably worried about appropriation. It is right and proper that writers should give this due consideration before embarking on a project. How terrible it would be if you sought to honour and recognise a particular culture and instead offended people who belonged to it. Personally, I think including characters from a range of backgrounds and cultures is essential to creating page-turning fiction for the 21st Century reader. Works that do not accurately represent our society feel dated and trite. But this aspect of writing must be approached with the deepest respect.

There are a few strategies you can use to ensure you show that due respect to other cultures and societal groups you may wish to represent in your stories. One quite simple way is to keep your writing firmly fixed in the third person. Write about people from all walks of life, but do so using 'he', 'she' and 'they'. This is much safer ground than using the first person 'I' which could be construed as you trying to speak directly for the people in that culture rather than bringing their challenges and successes into sharp focus in your story.

Another approach is to ensure you are not basing your fictional character on the specific journey of a particular individual from that community. This is risky. It can lead people to believe that you are taking a story that belongs to that community and using it for profit. Instead, I recommend reaching out to those communities you wish to represent as a whole. Ask them to talk about their culture, tell you stories. Read up on that culture. Watch documentaries. Listen to podcasts. Then, using all of that research, the various experiences, thoughts and feelings of the whole community, synthesise a new character who has faced their own challenges based on a more general overview of that culture's shared history. This process will ensure that you are not taking something concrete from that community for your own profit. Rather, you are using their collective experience as inspiration to create something new that will represent what you have learned about them.

The last point I'll make when it comes to avoiding appropriation, and thus making sure that your book is as representative and respectful as possible, is to consider giving something back to the communities and cultures you choose to include in your story. Two of my books (one novella and one poetry collection) raise money for the Native American Heritage Association. I had an American aunt marry into my English family in the late eighties and she had Apache ancestry. As a kid from the quiet catacombs of the North East, I was utterly enthralled by this lady and her tales of life across the ocean.

Given this youthful fascination, it's hardly surprising that Native American culture has woven its way into my writing as an adult but I wouldn't dream of putting a book inspired by this culture on the market without giving some of the proceeds to an appropriate charity. This, I believe, is fitting compensation for the inspiration that this culture affords me. Each year,

when I send the royalties along to the NAHA, I receive a lovely message of gratitude from them explaining that they are glad to be part of the inspiration for my work. These messages fill me with the utmost joy. It is what I hoped to create when I first thought about how I would sensitively represent their rich and fascinating culture. I want them to profit from the inspiration they extend to me, that seems only right.

C is for consent. This issue definitely comes under the dangerous stories we keep telling umbrella. On the surface it seems to me this aspect of writing fiction should be straightforward, but for some reason it gets people in a bit of a twist. Here's a golden rule: if a character says no to physical contact and another character ignores this or tries to verbally pressure the character into physical contact, this is not redeemable behaviour. I'm not here to tell you what to write, but if you wish to show the redemption of a character who doesn't heed the rules of consent I hope you're prepared to put the perpetrator through every available wringer.

Such a narrative is explored through the character of Spike in the TV show *Buffy the Vampire Slayer*. Spike attempts to rape Buffy in the season six episode *Seeing Red*. Whether his character is redeemed by the season seven finale is down to the individual viewer to decide. But any forgiveness he did receive was hard won. Immediately after the incident with Buffy, Spike is haunted by the memory of what he's done, runs away to Africa where he earns back his soul and ultimately sacrifices his life in a final battle. In short, there should be desperate consequences for assaulting a person, usually the price the character pays negates a Happily Ever After. Or, at least, a traditional one.

The characters in my own stories who exhibit unwanted sexually forceful behaviour do not win the heart of their victim or sympathy from other characters. I ensure this breach of trust serves as a clear signal to the protagonist that they should get as far away from this person as they can.

That they should instead seek out people who respect them, who will cherish them and care more about them than they do their own gratification. I don't believe in genre being an excuse on this score either. I have read historical romances that have carried this off perfectly – even in times when it was deemed a woman's duty to submit to the sexual desires of men. In those books, a distinction is made between the gentlemanly rogues and, well, characters that are essentially serial rapists. Regardless of the context, it is possible to deal with consent in a sensitive fashion.

Perhaps some of the confusion on this topic arises when exploring darker sensuality in our fiction. For example, some people find saying 'no' or struggling during a sexual encounter with a person they feel safe with tremendously erotic. But it's difficult to explore this kind of relationship responsibly without the appropriate set-up. If your characters are playing a dark, risky power game I say bravo and wish them all the pleasure in the world. But it is the author's responsibility to ensure it's clear that all parties involved are consenting to and enjoying this experience in a climate of mutual trust. Otherwise, we run the risk of reinforcing some very dangerous attitudes about romance and sexual practice. The 21st Century reader is not likely to have a lot of patience with authors who refuse to operate under more enlightened terms. There is a good chance it will mean that your story is put down and never picked up again. Check out my book *How to Write Sex* for more advice on this topic.

While the above acronym no doubt offers a useful reminder when thinking about how to best serve a modern-day reader, there are many subtleties not covered by this general approach. What is truly required is for writers to consider the climate these readers are living in, their sensitivities, their hopes and those things they despair of.

Even if your fiction is set a long time ago, issues relating to the modern experience of your readership will crop up. Careful thought needs to be given to how you will navigate those issues if you want to avoid alienating the people who have paid to read your work.

CHAPTER 10: THE UNREAL

For some reason, as fiction writers, we get it into our mind that the most important and worthy thing we can do is to emulate the real world down to the finest detail.

Why?

We're creating fiction, after all. Which by its very definition is not real life.

Sure, we want our writing to be laced with emotional truths that resonate with the reader but on the whole I would have to argue that an account of real life as we know it doesn't really make for the best fiction.

I would say, if anything, page-turning fiction has a distinct element of the unreal about it. As an example, take this blurb for my historical romance novella: *Once Upon a Rugged Knight*:

Maddie Dawson *has spent weeks looking forward to 'Once Upon a Dream', an annual Fairytale Convention in Nottingham. When a mysterious crone serves her a 'special cocktail' that looks dubiously like a magic potion however, she finds herself* transported to 1548, straight into the path of a beguiling but short-tempered knight who, it seems, is far from the gallant rescuer she is in need of.

Sir Pierce Carlyle should have been celebrating his engagement to **Lady Clarissa Bentley**. *Before he had a chance to propose, however, his rival,* **Lord Edmund Holtby,** *framed him for murder. Now he is on the run for his life. The last thing he needs is another problem. Yet that is exactly what he finds in Madelyn Dawson. She may be the most quick-tongued and sensual woman he has ever met, but he can tell just by looking at her unusual attire that she will be nothing but trouble.*

Cast out of their ordinary lives, Maddie and Sir Pierce strike a deal. She will help Sir Pierce to clear his name and teach him how to seduce his fair Clarissa. In exchange, he will deliver Maddie safely to an ancestor of the meddling crone who spirited her to the Tudor era, in the hope she can undo the spell. As their perilous journey unfolds however, Maddie and Sir Pierce begin to wonder if they were thrown across time, into each other's arms, for a reason. For what do decades and centuries mean when you are staring into the eyes of your true love?

I hope we can all agree that, at least on the surface, this story sounds nothing short of preposterous. When I uploaded this blurb to Amazon for preorders, I said to myself: 'this is the most bonkers thing I have ever written.'

And it is, but by my own admission my stories only get more bonkers the more of them I write. And yet my readership keeps growing...

Some writers would have looked at this blurb in black and white, live on the Amazon sales page, and had a moment of panic. *Is it too much?* They probably would have asked themselves. And depending on their purpose, they may have been right to do so.

My purpose, however, is to write stories that provide escape for my readers. Consequently, I was very comfortable with how silly my story sounded. Medieval Time-Travel is a popular romance subgenre, but it was obvious just by the ticks and quirks of the blurb that my story had elements that set it apart from others. For any of you wondering whether anyone would voluntarily hand over money for a book that sounds this ridiculous, I can tell you that at the time of writing it is still four months until the book's release and it is doing very well for preorders.

Will there be emotional truth to this story? Yes, bags of it. Maddie is going to the fairytale convention to take a break from caring for her sick mother. But is this story in any way 'realistic'? Goodness, no. I'm the first to admit that. But so long as writers deliver on the emotional truth of the situation, readers will often thank you for not being a slave to realism. They will be grateful to escape into a more extreme environment between the pages where the stakes are higher than those they usually grapple with and they can meet characters who struggle through adversity, just as they do.

In truth, reality is quite tedious at times. It often involves repetitive tasks or situations. Things don't always go our way. The daily news headlines can be overwhelming and fear-mongering. Thus, regardless of the genre you are writing in, I recommend injecting an element of the unreal. Yes, this even applies to literary work – assuming you want your literary work to be just as page-turning as a genre piece.

For a moment, let's move back along the spectrum of realism, away from the giddy extremes of my flighty imagination. Let's pretend you are writing a literary story about a couple who are about to be evicted from a flat they rent. That's something that many people face, it's realistic but in fiction, because we are trying to bring the reader into 'unreal' situations, we need to layer this with other elements of crisis. The last time I faced possible eviction from a flat, my husband had just been diagnosed with cancer. Mercifully, the landlady managed to find somewhere else to live, so she didn't have to evict us. But for a couple of months during chemotherapy, we didn't know if we'd have to look for a new home. So you could add that element into the story and still be within the bounds of realism, after all it happened to me.

There then comes the question: what extra layer could be added to this story to heighten the conflict to almost extreme proportions? Well, so far, the characters have only been subjected to external conflicts. For extra layers of conflict, perhaps we should now divert our attentions inward. How about, just before the cancer diagnosis, the husband asked his wife for a divorce? That's a pretty 'unreal' situation. I mean, I'm sure it has happened, but that's a lot of conflict to work through and would make the basis for a truly moving literary story.

You would need to explore what the transformation is for the characters, and for their relationship. Is the wife staying to support him through his cancer treatment out of duty, love or fear? Does the husband regret asking for a divorce now that the cancer diagnosis has given him perspective? Does this situation bring them closer together or push them further apart? It would depend what kind of book you wanted to write, what themes and messages you wanted to grapple with but layering conflict in this manner is essentially like putting your characters in a pressure cooker and waiting to see if they manage to establish a healthy simmer or boil over (tip – it's probably good if they boil over at some point).

Perhaps asking fiction writers to let go of realism doesn't seem like that big a deal when we are often creating fantastical worlds or scenarios. But it surprises me how many writers cling to it as though making their story realistic is the most important thing they can do for it. I'm here to reassure you that it's probably best to at the very least loosen your grip on reality when it comes to your written work. Realism is an overrated commodity even in scenarios on the page that don't involve dragons or magical time travel.

Though your work will undoubtedly incorporate real issues and real emotion, rather than writing a story and asking yourself 'does this seem real' a better question might be 'does this feel true?' Truth strikes to the heart of readers in a way that realism can never touch.

CHAPTER 11: DIALOGUE

Just like opening lines, people will tell you that your dialogue also has to 'work hard' for you whenever you are writing a story. Although this is as true for dialogue as it is for first lines, again it's rare to see anyone break down what is really meant by this.

For a start, and linking back to my argument in chapter ten, I'm afraid dialogue is not likely to work hard for you if you're trying too hard for realism. Have you ever listened to what the majority of actual people talk about as they're walking down the street? Of course not, you're far too polite to eavesdrop. Me too. But a far less polite friend once told me that while you might occasionally overhear some gem of a conversation, more often than not people are talking about what they need to buy from the grocery shop. Or what chores they need to get done when they get home. If they're feeling really wild, they might have a conversation about house prices.

In reality, people engage in small talk all the time but on the page there is little to no space for it, unless it is fulfilling one of the two primary functions of dialogue. The first being characterisation.

Most fiction writers are aware of the fact that dialogue serves a purpose when it comes to characterization. Unfortunately, they often rely on the same old elements of dialogue in order to develop that characterisation. For example, they will use contractions, slang or dialect to connote a person's class or social status. But there are so many more aspects of dialogue you can engage with in order to convey something important about your characters.

Sentence length is a big one that's always overlooked, and can be an efficient method of establishing conflict or comedic differences. If you create a scene in which a monosyllabic character meets a character whose sentences run on for three lines at a time, this is indicative of a meeting between two distinct personalities. The first person is guarded, aloof, and the second open and sociable. It wouldn't take very much to then construct reasons why these two characters behave this way and before you know it you've got a backstory. Just by manipulating the length of the sentences when your characters speak.

How a character's speech shifts depending on who they are talking to can also tell us a lot about them, while injecting additional drama or comedy. Ask yourself the following questions: who is your character trying to impress and how do they talk to them? Who does your character think they are 'better than' and how do they address them? Who will your character never speak to again? Who is your character dying to speak to but has never plucked up the courage?

How does their speech change depending on these different situations? Think about body language, the use of pauses and the word selection as you explore these elements of your story. Contemplating these elements of dialogue is pretty much guaranteed to add instant depth to your characters.

Additionally, you can juxtapose what the character thinks and what the character says on the page so the reader can, at once, gauge how open they are being about who they are and what their agenda is. Thoughts in fiction are usually italicised for emphasis and when they are placed right next to dialogue, particularly dialogue that contradicts what the character is thinking, it offers the reader a genuine sense of how authentic the character is being in this moment. You may use this technique to establish a character as untrustworthy but there are many other uses such as suggesting the character is withholding important information for another character's safety or protection. All of these elements, when varied as appropriate to your purpose, aid the development of characterization on the page.

The second most-common function of dialogue is to move the narrative forward. Or, in other words, to move the character closer to their ultimate transformation. To be clear: this doesn't mean that the characters should recite important plot information as though they are talking to camera. Or tell somebody else they are in a scene with something that person already knows. But they can discuss elements of their world and situation, alongside their thoughts, feelings and actions, all of which have the capacity to advance the plot depending on the genre you are writing in.

Often the best dialogue is serving a dual purpose. It develops our understanding of characterization and the plot simultaneously. With this in mind, it is always worth doing an edit of your stories where you look solely at the dialogue and make sure every exchange earns its place on the page. That it serves some function and isn't an indulgence of the writer.

An example of such an indulgence might be if the characters in a story have an in-depth discussion about Jungian psychology for no other purpose than it interests the author. Don't get me wrong, I think it's great you have interests. But it's a gamble that your reader shares that interest and if they don't you are doing nothing more but testing their patience. A far better approach is to make sure every conversation leads somewhere. One last note on dialogue relating, again, to the issue of realism discussed in the last chapter. Sometimes the most sparkling dialogue goes against expectation. It grabs us, entertains us and moves us because it neatly surprises us.

Take this dialogue from my all-time favourite book: The Princess *Bride* by William Goldman.

'You seem a decent fellow,' Inigo said. *'I hate to kill you.'*

'You seem a decent fellow,' answered the man in black. *'I hate to die.'*

Realistically, there is little chance that somebody would answer an aggressor the way the man in black answers Inigo and yet it is a charming and delightful exchange that not only surprises us but encapsulates the whole conflict at play in just two lines. The compassion Inigo shows to the man he is about to dispense of is surprising to us. This is in part because, in stories, kidnappers are usually portrayed in rather black and white terms with no compassion or personality other than they are the 'bad guy.'

The man in black's response is also surprising because on the surface it gives the impression that he assumes he will be bested while at the same time hinting to the reader that anyone with a response this dry must surely have a plan up their sleeves. In short, these characters speak against type and expectation. This is far more compelling than an obvious, stock response.

It may not be appropriate to your story and purpose to have characters quipping each other all the way through the narrative, but the example from *The Princess Bride* above was merely that: an example. There are lots of ways a person can respond counter to our expectations in a situation. Perhaps they take things more lightly than expected, or more seriously. Perhaps they take offence when we would not expect it. Perhaps they make a very dark-natured or threatening remark that the other characters might not see coming. When writing dialogue, one of the best questions we can ask ourselves once we're sure characterization and plot are in the bag is: *what kind of response is the reader expecting here and how can I reasonably manipulate that?*

If your dialogue is sparky, interesting or intriguing it will hook your reader. It will also cement your reputation for writing characters that go beyond the usual stock and stereotypes. I'm not sure about you, but I class both of these things as a big win.

CHAPTER 12: TELLING DETAILS

Throughout this volume I've analysed and deconstructed many a phrase that gets bandied around creative writing groups. I've been in enough of them, as both student and teacher, to know most of them by heart. But perhaps the most notorious of all is that well-worn phrase 'the telling details.'

If you've been writing for any length of time at all, someone at some point will have turned to you and said: 'This is good but I think it needs more telling details.'

But what does that mean and why are the telling details such an integral part of writing page-turning fiction?

Essentially, it comes down to this: when creating your characters you could just tell the reader that they were blonde or tall or broad. But that doesn't really convey anything specific about a character that will help them stick in the minds of your readers. For example, the fact that my librarian sleuth Kitt Hartley has little-else but work wear in her wardrobe tells the reader far more about her than the fact her hair is red. The fact that her hair is red is mentioned but that is used to offer a quick visual to the reader and I don't state all of her physical features at once so it sounds like a shopping list.

Often I will weave such basic, physical information into an action in a dialogue tag. Hopefully, the difference between an arbitrary detail and a telling detail is evident here. A telling detail tells us something more intimate about the character. The fact that Kitt Hartley's wardrobe is full of work wear tells us that she might be something of a workaholic or at the very least needs to get out more. The fact that she has red hair tells us… that she was born with red hair. When writing, I spend a little more time on the telling details for the simple reason that they carry more weight for both the reader and the story.

The same approach can be used when describing setting. Your character may well have a mahogany dining table. But is it polished every day by a maid? Or is it scratched and scuffed? Was it picked up second-hand because your character couldn't afford anything else at the time?

Hopefully, you can already see the difference between listing physical details and offering carefully-selected telling details to the reader. One of them quickly establishes an image in the minds of your readers. The other insinuates truths about the character on a more subtle level.

Most of the time it is better to be sparing with the physical details and generous with the telling details, but there are exceptions to this advice. If you're setting up a series for example, you may want to offer the reader a lot of physical detail in book one so that in book two you can just refer to the living room or the library, perhaps dropping in a couple of cursory reminders of odd details, and your readers will already know what that place looks like thanks to your in-depth description in the first book. I did this in my first cosy mystery novel and although one or two reviewers complained that they didn't want that much detail, the majority of reviewers understood what I was doing and were glad of the information that, they knew, would serve them as the series continued.

Some people only use the telling details in their work. So you might find out that a character's most prized possession is a locket that their mother gave them, but never find out their hair is brown. Personally, I love stories like this. I think it prompts readers to visualise their own physical versions of those characters rather than have that dictated by the author. I also like the fact that readers are encouraged to build their impressions of characters on non-physical terms. I must stress however that, given reader feedback over the years, I am in a minority. Most readers want to quickly establish a person's physical features early on, alongside their age, and it is thus down to the author to find inventive ways of weaving them into the story without slowing down the action. Lacing your stories with appropriate telling details however will make your characters and settings resonate with your readers at a much deeper level. Without realising it's even happening, readers will come to know the people who inhabit your story much more intimately and anything that enhances the bond between your readers and your characters can only be a good thing.

CHAPTER 13: WALK AND CHEW GUM

There are some genre exceptions to this guideline but on the whole I have learnt that stories are much harder for the reader to put down if more than one thing is happening at a time. Or, to put it another way, if you are stimulating your reader in more than one way at once.

Let's take the example of two criminals meeting before a heist in a suspense novel. You could get them to meet anywhere. An abandoned warehouse is traditional. Which means it's been done and it would be much more stimulating to the reader if you chose somewhere else for them to meet.

What if they got on the big wheel at a fairground to discuss their business? What if they met on a cruise ship? Or in the middle of the dessert? At once, this makes for more stimulating reading because the sole function of the scene is no longer just conveying their business. It is also portraying how the characters navigate the pleasures and hazards of this environment, which in turn teaches us more about them as people. If you wanted to make the setting a telling detail and add some foreshadowing or intrigue into the proceedings, you could have one criminal ask the other *'why did you choose to meet here, of all places?'* How the other criminal responds is up to you. Maybe there's some dark personal reason we don't find out about until later. Maybe it's an opportunity for it to be clarified that one criminal doesn't question the other criminal. Whatever the response, your story is working for readers on another level if you include this kind of stimulation.

Let's fast forward now to the heist. The two criminals are about to enter the bank or jewellery store or the museum or wherever it is they are going to rob. You could choose this moment to let the two characters have a conversation about something important or you could start the scene as they enter the building. The conversation will then be interspersed with all the actions they are carrying out to complete the heist (side note: it's not a good idea to write a story in which a character is on their own all the time. It becomes a very internal, intellectual narrative rather than an active one. Giving your character somebody to talk to about whatever crisis they are facing is usually much safer ground.).

Structuring your action in the manner modelled above, particularly in act one and act two of your story, can prevent paragraphs from feeling like lists of tasks the characters complete but also means the story doesn't have to slow down just because the characters are having a conversation.

Essentially, this is an extension of the 'arrive late, leave early' rule outlined earlier. By starting the scene at the point in which the characters are having a conversation we sometimes fail to bring the reader in when the action really starts. As most conversations can be had 'on the run' it makes sense to combine the two so that the story can move at a swifter pace.

In act three, you may find it is more prudent to ease off with this technique because often we are building towards some huge showdown with the antagonist the characters have been fighting against all the way through the story. In these sequences you may wish to increase the ratio of action to dialogue considerably to build momentum and to give the reader a powerful impression of whatever the climactic battle may comprise. This caveat largely applies to genres such as fantasy, action, suspense, spy and thriller stories where the ultimate climax is physical, and often a fight scene. In romances and mysteries, the climaxes are usually more dialogue- heavy and thus you would circle back to thinking about how setting could be used as extra stimulation during the climax. Where is the most interesting place for a character to declare undying love? Or unmask a killer?

And speaking of declaring undying love or unmasking killers, romances and mysteries are books in which your reader might thank you for slowing down the pace and fixating on just one form of stimulation at a time in the odd chapter here and there. As explained in chapter two, considerations of genre are always paramount when constructing a piece of fiction and I know that my cosy mystery readers are thrilled if my librarian sleuth stops to have a cup of tea and chat over the latest clues. Of course, I try to make the backdrop to that cuppa as interesting as I can, but it's hardly a heist- in-progress situation. And my readers are OK with that because the cosy reader likes a gentle breather between action sequences. Likewise, romance readers will be happier if sometimes you fixate only on the couple being together rather than forwarding any grand plot. So walk and chew gum, yes, as is appropriate to the story you are writing.

CHAPTER 14: PAGE-TURNING SUPERPOWER

Did you know that authors of page-turning fiction have a very special super power?

No, it's not the power to make politicians tell the truth. That would be useful though.

It's invisibility.

Essentially, writers of page-turning fiction create such an immersive experience that readers forget they are even reading the story. How does a writer achieve that? Well, all the advice that has preceded this chapter is the best starting point I can offer you but there are a couple of other things we do, terrible habits really, that can snap a reader out of their story-trance (official term, honest) in an instant.

The first is a matter of word choice. Sometimes we writers get concerned that readers might not know how clever we are. I don't know why we worry about this but I know we do because for no good reason whatsoever we'll insert an eight-syllable word where a two syllable one would have sufficed into what was, until that point, a perfectly immersive story. When we do this however, we may as well pop out of the page, waving our arms at readers while shouting *'Hey, hey you there! I'm really, really clever and you're reading my story.'*

This is bad enough if it happens once in the space of a story, but if it happens multiple times there is a strong likelihood that the reader will lose patience with our persistent and distracting ego trips. I concede we don't always engage in this behaviour for the sole purpose of making ourselves look clever. Sometimes we just really love a word. I love the word mellifluous, but I'm not convinced I've found room for it in one of my stories yet. Whether it's about making ourselves look clever or using the words we like rather than using what is a best fit for that story, can we at least agree it is a writer indulgence that we should probably, if possible, resist? The reader likely already respects us enough for writing a story in the first place without us resorting to tactics such as these.

Another habit that is good to avoid if you want to employ your page turning author super power and remain invisible is including obscure literary references in your work without offering enough context for them to remain accessible. It's great that your character knows so much about *The Odyssey*, but some of us were raised on nothing more lofty than the latest episode of *Knight Rider,* and if we're to understand what you're talking about, you need to give us an inroad into your work.

In the early stages of my writing career, I was as guilty of this as any other writer. In my case, it was a result of an insecurity about the fact I came from a working class background. I wanted to show the world I'd read the important stuff I was supposed to, even though I didn't attend a swanky school or get outstanding grades. It took a while for me to realise that telling a story wasn't supposed to be a test of intellect for myself or the reader. Once I got that straight in my head, I did just fine. This advice doesn't mean, by the way, that you should never reference other literature in your books.

My first novel featured an ex-English teacher as the chief character (I'm an ex- English teacher myself, but no relation). This character was big on her literary references. I also write cosy mysteries about a crime- solving librarian who uses other plots in fiction to help her solve the mystery (most of the time not all that successfully). The difference between these examples and the references I used earlier in my career is that now I always provide the necessary context so that readers can access the story whether they've heard of the works I'm referring to. My expectation isn't that my readers have the same to-be-read pile as my protagonists, or me.

The last thing I'm going to comment on when it comes to making yourself invisible is your use of literary devices within your work. My advice would be to use metaphors, similes and such sparingly. A few people will even clobber you in the review box for that much, but I think most readers appreciate the odd well-placed metaphor so long as it doesn't slow down the pace of the book. If you look back at your story after reading this chapter and find it is packed with almost nothing but literary devices then, even if it is a literary novel, I would advise getting the red pen out and making some hard choices about which images are the most striking and thus worth keeping.

As much as I love imagery-rich prose, when a piece of writing is laden down with too many examples it feels heavy, repetitive and slow. I understand this is a painful thing for writers to hear. It pained me when I first learned it for myself. For what writer doesn't love words, and the ways in which we can manipulate them so beautifully on a page just for the sake of it? Learning this truth is probably what made me finally understand how to write poetry properly. I had to find a space where I could revel in those intricate linguistic features.

But when it comes to writing fiction those feelings of the story seeming heavy, repetitive and slow, just aren't conducive to getting readers to turn pages. So, I suppose in a nutshell, this ex-English teacher is asking you to forget a lot of what you learned in English class about what makes good writing. A metaphor might be beautiful in its own right, but a story is not built with metaphors. It is built with characters navigating difficult situations and that is always, always the priority over ornate language.

I know. The truth really hurts sometimes.

CHAPTER 15: THE EDITORIAL PROCESS

Given the title of this book, I have focussed almost entirely on the process of writing fiction. I'm pretty sure you'd feel a little bit short changed and may even have written to me about a suggested title change for this volume if I hadn't. But it is safe to say that many of the page-turning elements of your story are more likely to ripen during the developmental editing process. As Michael Crichton once said: *'Books aren't written, they're rewritten.'* And the same is actually true of stories of any length. For only once you have a full, raw first draft can you look at the story as a whole and assess its capacity to excite, delight and make fans out of readers.

A good starting point is to read your story over once while shifting into the mind-set of a discerning reader or editor. On this first read through, you are looking for any moments in the story when you start to lose interest or even, dare I say it, get bored. As pointed out earlier, if a story bores you, it will bore a reader. Mark those up so you know to return to them. You simply do not have room for sections like that if you want this to be a story that your readers can't put down.

Once you've completed a pass like this, it's time to use the tools and tricks in this book to try and jazz up those moments that don't strike you as the most compelling. In some cases, you will be able to rewrite them in a more captivating manner, applying the techniques outlined in previous chapters.

In other cases, you will no doubt have to concede that the reason it's boring is because it doesn't need to be in this story. That's always a hard lump to swallow and is what the time-worn phrase 'kill your darlings' is all about. Because yes, I can almost guarantee that the bits you realise you have to cut will be your absolute favourites of all the bits you've written. In a way, that's probably part of the reason they need to be cut. If you love them so much there was a chance you were indulging yourself rather than serving the reader in that part of the story. But don't worry. It's totally fine to do that in a first draft. You were having fun. You were experimenting. And after you cut them from the pages of your story, you still have them to look back on and enjoy. And if you develop a really hungry fan base you can share your 'deleted scenes' with them as an extra bonus through a mailing list or via social media. Those are the places for the bits you love but have to cut. They don't, I'm afraid, belong in your story.

After that, I recommend taking several more passes at your work focusing only on one thing at a time. If you read this way, your edits are guaranteed to be thorough because you can give all your energy and focus to that one element of storytelling. If you notice other faults as you go, just mark or highlight them to address at a later date. But as you read, stay fixed on whatever element you've selected on each pass. Focusing on the element of structure first, before getting into smaller details, is often a strong next step at this stage. Try addressing the following points:

Is there a clear transformation across the whole story?

Is there a clear transformation within each chapter or scene?

Does each chapter or scene employ the 'arrive late, leave early' rule?

Do the last lines of each chapter end on a note of uncertainty?

Is there more than one source of stimulation in every scene or chapter?

Following that, you might find it useful to focus on dialogue while addressing the following points:

Does each conversation lead the characters forward in their transformation?

Are both characterization and plot being moved forward simultaneously with each line?

Are any of the responses obvious, trite or stock phrases?

Is there a contrast between what characters say and what they think?

How are pauses and body language used for effect?

Does the rhythm and word choice for each character match their background?

Does the sentence length of each line match that character's disposition?

Lastly, I recommend analysing your use of description while asking

the following questions:

Have I used longer words where shorter words will do? Have I used three adjectives where one will suffice?

How many literary devices have I used and are they all earning their place on the page? Are any repetitive or cliché?

Have I woven basic physical details into my story in a non-obtrusive manner?

Have I offered the reader telling details which will offer a deeper sense of the character or setting?

Once you have completed these phases of the editing process, you will have taken a lot more care over polishing your story than many others who settle for the first thing they write without questioning its strengths or areas for improvement. And so long as you have been honest with yourself throughout this process and haven't dodged any rewrites, your story should be ready to send off to an editor, agent or competition as appropriate to whatever stage you have reached on your writing journey. For if you have employed all the advice offered and taken notes of any caveats, then congratulations are in order. Because there is a very good chance that you have just finished writing a piece of page-turning fiction.

If you enjoyed this book, please consider leaving a review.

ACKNOWLEDGEMENTS

Heartfelt thanks to the many creative writing students I have connected with over the years who encouraged me to write this book and convinced me it was something writers out there needed.

Thank you to Ann Leander for her editorial work on this book and to Dean Cummings for his ongoing support for my writing journey. Gratitude also to Hammad Khalid for designing this volume and to the many authors who have inspired me, far too numerous to name individually, over my years of writing stories.

About the Author

Helen Cox is a Yorkshire-born novelist and poet. After completing her MA in creative writing at the University of York St. John Helen wrote for a range of publications, edited her own independent film magazine for five years and penned three non-fiction books.

Her first two novels were published by HarperCollins in 2016. She currently lives by the sea in Sunderland where she writes poetry, romance novellas, and The Kitt Hartley series alongside hosting The Poetrygram podcast. You can find out more about Helen's work at HelenCoxBooks.Com

ADVICE TO AUTHORS SERIES

How & When to Sign a Book Deal
How to Become a Published Writer
How to Write Sex
How & When to Quit Your Day Job

www.ingramcontent.com/pod-product-compliance
Lightning Source LLC
Chambersburg PA
CBHW050507120526
44588CB00044B/1666